THE U.S. GOVERNMENT
HOW IT WORKS

THE HISTORY OF
THE REPUBLICAN PARTY

THE U.S. GOVERNMENT
HOW IT WORKS

★ ★ ★

THE U.S. GOVERNMENT
HOW IT WORKS

THE HISTORY OF THE REPUBLICAN PARTY

HEATHER LEHR WAGNER

CHELSEA HOUSE
PUBLISHERS
An imprint of Infobase Publishing

The History of the Republican Party

Chelsea House
An imprint of Infobase Publishing
132 West 31st Street
New York NY 10001

Library of Congress Cataloging-in-Publication Data
Wagner, Heather Lehr.
  The history of the Republican party / Heather Lehr Wagner.
      p. cm. — (The U.S. government : how it works)
  Includes bibliographical references and index.
  ISBN-13: 978-0-7910-9417-4 (hardcover)
  ISBN-10: 0-7910-9417-0 (hardcover)
  1. Republican Party (U.S. : 1854-)—History.   2. United States—Politics and government.   I. Title.
  JK2356.W25 2007
  324.273409—dc22

                                        2006101967

Series design by James Scotto-Lavino
Cover design by Ben Peterson

Printed in the United States of America
Bang NMSG 10 9 8 7 6 5 4 3 2 1

This book is printed on acid-free paper.

All links and Web addresses were checked and verified to be correct at the time of publication. Because of the dynamic nature of the Web, some addresses and links may have changed since publication and may no longer be valid.

CONTENTS

1

THE BIRTH OF THE REPUBLICAN PARTY

The United States that existed in the 1850s was a nation united in name only. By then, disputes over many issues bitterly divided America. The nation had not yet celebrated 100 years of independence, and the guiding principles of government that were once so clearly defined had withered in the face of new issues that claimed the public's attention. These controversies would soon plunge the nation into civil war.

The chaos that marked America at this period in its history is often attributed to a single subject: slavery. Slavery certainly was at the forefront of the national debate, particularly as new states joined the union and western territories were opened up for settlement. Other, equally contentious matters also separated one American from another, however.

By the middle of the nineteenth century, large waves of immigrants were pouring into America. Nearly 3 million immigrants arrived in America between 1845 and 1854, a number that represented more than 14 percent of the country's total population, according to William E. Gienapp's book, *The Origins of the Republican Party*. Prejudice against foreigners, particularly Catholic foreigners, soon followed. In 1850, a political party was formed specifically to give a political platform to this anti-Catholic, antiforeigner ideology. Its name was the Order of the Star-Spangled Banner, but party members were given the nickname "Know Nothings" because members were told that, if anyone asked about the party, they were to say that they knew nothing about it.

Yet another issue of political importance, particularly in individual states, was the debate over alcohol. A temperance movement (a movement that called for the strict regulation or outright banning of sales of alcoholic beverages) had divided political parties in Maine and soon spread to other states. Politicians and their supporters were forced to take a public position on alcohol regulation.

Other issues sparked additional debate: How and when should businesses be regulated? Should support be given to free enterprise? Should businesses be closed on Sundays? Should public funds be given to religious schools? Should prayer be included in public schools? Many of the issues that still mark political discussions today first appeared in the nineteenth century.

Political parties played a critical role in shaping these debates and formulating responses to the issues that mattered to the majority of Americans. Most Americans voted along strict party lines—most American white males, that is, as neither women nor African Americans had the right to vote. A person's political party was less a reflection of his support for a particular candidate and far more a reflection of his family background, job, and position in society. Candidates for higher office were selected by the political parties. Voters assumed that, if a particular candidate had been chosen as the representative of a particular political party, then he would thoroughly reflect that party's positions and attitudes.

Despite the rise of certain small political parties like the "Know Nothings," America was essentially a nation of two political parties. In the first half of the nineteenth century, those two parties were the Democratic Party and the Whig Party.

COLLAPSE OF THE WHIG PARTY

The Whig Party had become a powerful political force in the United States in the 1830s as a response to the strong presidency of Democrat Andrew Jackson. Many Americans were opposed to the idea of a powerful president, preferring that the individual states retain more power. This was an issue that had divided America from its very

Andrew Jackson's status as military hero following the War of 1812 translated into political support during his two terms as president.

beginning, when the Founding Fathers debated how much power should be held by the states and how much should be given to the national government.

President Jackson expanded the powers of the Executive Branch, in large part through his use of the presidential veto power. Through his use of the veto against any legislation with which he disagreed, it became clear that the Executive Branch could quickly become more powerful than the Legislative Branch (Congress).

The Whig Party took its name from the Whig Party in Great Britain, which was opposed to an overly powerful monarchy. The Whigs in America supported a more powerful Congress and also focused on issues of modernization and economic development. The party soon overtook the Democratic Party in urban areas, particularly in the northern United States. Two Whig candidates were elected to the presidency: William Henry Harrison in 1841 and Zachary Taylor in 1849. Both men died in office. Vice President John Tyler, who became president when Harrison died, quickly vetoed many of the Whig platform issues and was forced out of the party. With Zachary Taylor's death, Vice President Millard Fillmore became president. He would be the last Whig to serve as president, and during his term in office he signed the Fugitive Slave Act, which offered federal officers' assistance to slaveholders who sought to recapture runaway slaves. This issue would bitterly divide Whigs, and, by the 1852 presidential election, the party positions on slavery and many other critical issues of the day were no longer clear and unified.

Former Whigs split off; some joined the Democrats and others joined new parties like the Know Nothings or the

Free Soil Party, which opposed the extension of slavery into western territories. It soon became clear, however, that a political party organized around a single issue would have only limited appeal, drawing votes only from those who felt most strongly about that particular issue. A new political party was needed, a party that would provide a unified platform to address the many issues that were dividing the nation, a party that would represent a change from the past but whose positions would be solid enough to appeal to a large number of Americans.

A NEW FORCE

The Republican Party first rose to power on local and state levels rather than the national stage. It is thought to have been founded in Ripon, Wisconsin, on the night of March 20, 1854. A group of Whigs, Free Soilers, and Democrats met at a schoolhouse to create a party that accurately reflected their views on government. They chose the name "Republican" to show their ties to Thomas Jefferson's Democratic-Republican Party (which had briefly been known as the Republican Party when it was founded). Jefferson's party had supported states' rights, a strict interpretation of the Constitution, and a decentralized national government with limited powers. (The Democratic-Republican Party evolved into the Democratic Party under Andrew Jackson.)

Between the first informal gathering in Ripon, Wisconsin, and the first formal meeting in Jackson, Michigan, a few months later, the political philosophy of the new

This scene on a cotton plantation gives an indication of life in the American South in the nineteenth century. One of the issues that united the Republican Party of the 1850s was its strong antislavery stance.

Republican Party became clear. Perhaps the key issue at the time was an opposition to the spread of slavery into the western territories of Kansas and Nebraska, as would be allowed under the federal government's Kansas-Nebraska Act.

It is important to note that many Whigs initially resisted joining the Republican Party. Illinois senator Abraham Lincoln, elected as a Whig Party candidate in 1854, felt that the Republicans were too radical. Other Whig supporters felt that only an established political party could hold the country together and keep slavery in check.

Slowly, support for the Republican Party grew. Republican candidates won state elections in Maine, Vermont, Ohio, Wisconsin, Indiana, and Michigan in 1854. As the collapse of the Whig Party became evident, Lincoln and other prominent political figures agreed to join the new party. Free Soilers, Democrats, and Know Nothings, as well as Whigs, helped ensure that this new party was more a coalition than a single-issue organization. The party represented a number of clear political positions: antislavery, conservative economic programs marked by high tariffs on imported goods, and rapid development of the West by government-supported homesteading.

In 1856, the Republican Party held its first presidential nomination convention in Philadelphia. The candidate they chose was John C. Frémont, a leading figure in the exploration of the West who had earned the nickname "the Pathfinder" for his adventures. The political platform of the new Republican Party was reflected in a campaign that called for Congress to ban slavery in the western territories and in its slogan: "Free labor, free speech, free men, free Kansas, and Frémont."

Despite the fact that his party was new to the national scene, Frémont did surprisingly well, winning two-fifths of the electoral votes and carrying 11 states in the North. Measuring the strengths and failings of the election, party organizers believed that they had focused perhaps too heavily on the slavery issue and resolved to focus, in the Northern states that they had failed to carry, on the issues that spoke most directly to those voters. Tariffs on imports were emphasized in industrial and mining regions. Support for homesteaders was emphasized in regions where that issue was the principal focus of political debate.

THE SENATOR FROM ILLINOIS

As the 1860 presidential election drew near, the question of who would represent the Republican ticket became increasingly important. New York senator William Seward, one of the first prominent Whigs to join the Republicans, had risen to leadership within the party and was a logical choice for a presidential nominee. The Republicans had failed to carry Pennsylvania in 1856, and an argument was made for Senator Simon Cameron of Pennsylvania to be the Republicans' candidate for the presidency. Others suggested Ohio governor Salmon P. Chase, a former Democrat who, it was believed, might be able to pull Democratic support to the Republican ticket. Edward Bates of Missouri, the Speaker of the House, had strong support from many for his national prominence and legislative experience. Then there was Illinois senator Abraham Lincoln, who had gained attention for his series of debates with Stephen Douglas in 1858, when Douglas had attempted—unsuccessfully—to challenge Lincoln for the Senate.

The debate over where the Republican convention would be held reflected the competing support for the different candidates. Seward supporters argued for New York City; Chase supporters felt that Cleveland or Columbus was the appropriate choice; St. Louis was the choice for supporters of Bates. The secretary of the Republican

National Committee (RNC), a man named Norman Judd, argued that Chicago was a logical compromise choice, because (as Judd suggested) it was the one city that did not have a strong candidate for the presidency.

Judd was actually a friend of Abraham Lincoln's, and, once the Republican Party officials had agreed to the choice of Chicago, Judd arranged it so that he would be responsible for seating guests at the convention. Seward was considered the most likely choice for the presidential nomination, but, by the time New York delegates arrived at the convention, they found that most of the seats were already occupied—by local citizens from Chicago. When Seward's name was put into nomination, a large crowd cheered. The Chicagoans, determined not be outdone by New Yorkers, jumped on their seats and stamped, screamed, whistled, and cheered when the name of "their" candidate, Abraham Lincoln, was put into nomination. It quickly became clear that Lincoln, viewed only as a marginal candidate at best or more likely as a possible choice for vice president, needed to be taken seriously. He polled second (after Seward) in electoral votes in the first ballot and received twice as many as Cameron, Chase, or Bates.

Lincoln was not at the convention; he was awaiting news of the results in his hometown of Springfield, Illinois. His campaign team approached the supporters of Simon Cameron and suggested that, if Cameron would swing his support—and his delegates—to Lincoln, Cameron might be given a post in the Lincoln administration (Cameron would eventually become Lincoln's secretary

Abraham Lincoln *(above)* was relatively unknown when he was nominated as the Republican candidate for president in 1860.

of war). Cameron agreed, and, on the second ballot, the Pennsylvania delegates switched to Lincoln. By the third ballot, Lincoln had earned enough electoral votes to be nominated.

In the 1860 presidential election, Republican candidate Abraham Lincoln faced a Democratic Party divided by the slavery issue. Northern and Southern divisions of the Democratic Party nominated their own candidates—Stephen A. Douglas from the North and John C. Breckenridge from the South. Lincoln received only 40 percent of the popular vote but captured the presidency nonetheless, winning 60 percent of the electoral votes and 18 Northern states.

In only the second presidential election after its creation, the Republican Party had won the presidency. The victory would prove costly for Lincoln, however: By the time he was inaugurated as president, seven Southern states had seceded from the Union, and in 1861, the country he had pledged to lead would be torn apart by the Civil War.

2

CIVIL WAR
POLITICS

The first Republican president, Abraham Lincoln, was elected on November 6, 1860. Between the date of his election and the date of his inauguration—March 4, 1861— the country he had been chosen to lead started to crumble away. On December 20, 1860, South Carolina announced its intention to secede (separate) from the United States; soon, other Southern states were joining the movement.

As soon as he took office, Lincoln concentrated his efforts on preserving the Union—ensuring that the country did not disintegrate but remained one nation. The Republican Party, which had become identified with the antislavery movement, now became clearly identified as the "party of the Union."

To help ensure that his party, at least, was unified, Lincoln appointed to his cabinet the men who had been his rivals at the presidential convention: William H. Seward as secretary of state, Edward Bates as attorney general, Simon Cameron as secretary of war, and Salmon P. Chase as secretary of the treasury.

Initially, Lincoln and his advisers believed that the secession movement would be short-lived, even when the newly formed Confederate States of America elected Jefferson Davis as president on February 8, 1861. Then Confederate forces attacked Fort Sumter, and President Lincoln issued a call for volunteers to serve in the conflict.

The outbreak of war sparked new disagreements in the Republican Party. Some felt that Lincoln was acting too cautiously, not aggressively taking action to demonstrate the authority of the federal government. Defeats in battle sparked additional criticism of Lincoln's military leadership.

On September 22, 1862, Lincoln issued his preliminary Emancipation Proclamation. In this speech, he stated that "... on the first day of January ... all persons held as slaves within any State, or designated part of a State, the people whereof shall then be in rebellion against the United States, shall be then, thenceforward, and forever free." This speech essentially warned Confederate states that, if they did not stop fighting and rejoin the Union by January 1, 1863, all slaves in their states would be free. There was political maneuvering behind this speech. Lincoln was under pressure from those firmly opposed to slavery within his party, but he also knew that troops in southern Ohio, Indiana, Illinois, and Kentucky were protesting the idea of fighting a war to end slavery.

When the date of January 1, 1863, arrived and the nation was entering its third year of civil war, Lincoln followed up with the formal Emancipation Proclamation, stating that "all persons held as slaves" within the Confederate states "are, and henceforward shall be free." It is important to note that this proclamation applied only to slaves held in states that had seceded from the Union; slaves held in border states that had supported the Union were not freed. It also, of course, depended on a Union victory in the Civil War in order for the proclamation to be enforced.

The modern Republican Party proudly announces itself as the "party of Lincoln," but Republicans of Lincoln's time were in no way unanimously willing to affiliate themselves with the president. Defeats of Union forces in the war, ongoing questions about slavery, the high rate of casualties, the higher taxes forced by war expenses, and disagreements about the central issues of the war contributed to Republicans' lack of support for their incumbent president when the presidential election of 1864 drew near.

Lincoln's secretary of the treasury, Salmon P. Chase, mounted a brief effort to challenge Lincoln for the presidential nomination. His supporters represented a wing of the Republican Party also known as "Republican Radicals," who opposed making any concessions to the South in order to achieve peace. The Radicals also strongly felt

EMANCIPATION PROCLAMATION

★ ★ ★

On January 1, 1863, Abraham Lincoln issued the Emancipation Proclamation. The Civil War was nearing its third year when Lincoln signed the document that stated that all slaves held in the Confederate states "are, and henceforward shall be free":

> . . . Now, therefore I, Abraham Lincoln, President of the United States, by virtue of the power in me vested as Commander-in-Chief, of the Army and Navy of the United States in time of actual armed rebellion against the authority and government of the United States, and as a fit and necessary war measure for suppressing said rebellion, do, on this first day of January, in the year of our Lord one thousand eight hundred and sixty-three, and in accordance with my purpose so to do publicly proclaimed for the full period of one hundred days, from the day first above mentioned, order and designate as the States and parts of States wherein the people thereof respectively, are this day in rebellion against the United States, the following, to wit:

> Arkansas, Texas, Louisiana, (except the Parishes of St. Bernard, Plaquemines, Jefferson, St. John, St. Charles, St. James Ascension, Assumption, Terrebonne, Lafourche, St. Mary, St. Martin, and Orleans, including the City of New Orleans) Mississippi, Alabama, Florida, Georgia, South Carolina, North Carolina, and Virginia, (except the forty-eight counties designated as West Virginia, and also the counties of Berkley, Accomac, Northampton, Elizabeth City, York, Princess Ann, and Norfolk, including the

cities of Norfolk and Portsmouth[)], and which excepted parts, are for the present, left precisely as if this proclamation were not issued.

And by virtue of the power, and for the purpose aforesaid, I do order and declare that all persons held as slaves within said designated States, and parts of States, are, and henceforward shall be free; and that the Executive government of the United States, including the military and naval authorities thereof, will recognize and maintain the freedom of said persons.

And I hereby enjoin upon the people so declared to be free to abstain from all violence, unless in necessary self-defence; and I recommend to them that, in all cases when allowed, they labor faithfully for reasonable wages.

And I further declare and make known, that such persons of suitable condition, will be received into the armed service of the United States to garrison forts, positions, stations, and other places, and to man vessels of all sorts in said service.

And upon this act, sincerely believed to be an act of justice, warranted by the Constitution, upon military necessity, I invoke the considerate judgment of mankind, and the gracious favor of Almighty God. . . .

Source: www.archives.gov/exhibits/featured_documents/emancipation_proclamation/transcript.html.

Salmon P. Chase *(above)* opposed Lincoln during his first campaign, and even attempted to challenge Lincoln in his campaign for reelection. Despite this, Lincoln appointed Chase as secretary of the treasury during his first term, and nominated Chase as chief justice of the Supreme Court during his second term.

that slavery should be abolished throughout the Union and that African Americans should be given full political and social rights. In his cabinet post, Chase also benefited from the support of many powerful financial leaders. Surprisingly, Lincoln did not immediately ask Chase to resign from the cabinet when he began his campaign to unseat the president. Lincoln was determined to hold together not only the Union, but the Republican Party as well. To help underscore this, the party was now referred to as the National Union Party or Union Party.

Supporters of the Chase candidacy soon found that the president was far more popular than their candidate, but the wise Lincoln made a shrewd political move designed to please the members of his party who had expressed their displeasure with his policies by supporting an opponent. Lincoln suggested to the chairman of the Republican National Committee that, at the party convention, he propose a constitutional amendment to abolish slavery forever. The party platform also called for plans to encourage foreign immigration and the rapid construction of a railroad to the Pacific Coast.

Lincoln was ultimately the unanimous choice of the Republican convention of 1864. Only one state's delegates voted for another candidate—Missouri's delegates initially voted for the commander of the Union Army, General Ulysses S. Grant, before being persuaded to make the vote for Lincoln unanimous. The governor of Tennessee—a former tailor named Andrew Johnson—was chosen as Lincoln's running mate. Perhaps more significant than the fact that Johnson was from a border state is the fact that he was a Democrat, although he had remained fiercely loyal to the Union.

As their candidate, the Democrats chose General George McClellan, who was an officer in the Union Army. Despite the fact that the Democratic Party was being led by a Union general, the platform called for an immediate end to the war, with a convention of the states to be held afterward. It did not indicate whether there would be any specific conditions to this end of the conflict, such as the South agreeing to rejoin the Union. This uncertainty was coupled with suggestions that the Democrats were traitors to the Union. The term *Copperhead* was applied to Democrats who supported this policy of a negotiated settlement with the South; the term refers to a snake that sneaks up to its prey and strikes without warning. This suggestion of disloyalty to the Union would ultimately doom Democratic efforts to win the presidency.

THE PARTY AFTER LINCOLN

The direction Lincoln provided for the Republican Party ended on April 15, 1865, when the president was assassinated. Shortly before Lincoln's death, the Civil War had ended. Lincoln's assassination and the end of the Civil War marked a new era for the Republican Party. The party had struggled to remain unified even under Lincoln's skillful leadership, but patriotism helped ensure that the squabbling was minimized.

Now that the war had ended, however, it was no longer considered unpatriotic to criticize the president or his

A veteran in uniform sits in front of the Confederate flag
(above). After the Civil War, this flag was known as the
Conquered Banner.

policies. Lincoln's plan for the end of the Civil War was
clear: He believed that restraint should be used in helping the Southern states to rebuild. He did not want the

rebellious states to be crushed, nor did he want the federal government to assume any power over the Southern states that it had not held before the war began.

Andrew Johnson became president after Lincoln's assassination. He faced two immediate hurdles, at least in the eyes of Republican leaders: He was a Democrat, and he was from a Southern state. Two Republican congressional leaders decided to challenge Johnson. One was Senator Charles Sumner, who strongly believed that the war had been fought to free the slaves. Now that the war was over, former slaves must immediately be given the right to vote. It was the job of the federal government, Sumner believed, to force all state governments to immediately create equality.

In the House of Representatives was Thaddeus Stevens, a 74-year-old congressman from Pennsylvania who had long been publicly opposed to slavery. He felt that Lincoln's plan for postwar recovery (known as Reconstruction) of the Union was too timid. The Union had won; the Confederates states had lost. Now these former Confederate states should be told what to do.

It is important to note that Johnson was not opposed to ensuring that freed slaves were given the right to vote, nor was he a secret supporter of the Confederate cause, as some had charged. He felt, however, that he had a responsibility to follow through on the plan carefully crafted by Lincoln; he also believed that change (including instituting new voting policies) should proceed slowly, giving the states and citizens time to become accustomed to new policies and new regulations.

Andrew Johnson, vice president under Abraham Lincoln,
assumed the presidency after Lincoln was assassinated.
Johnson's background proved to be an obstacle to progress,
however: He was from a Southern state, and he was a
Democrat, two qualities seen as offensive by Republicans.

Both Stevens and Sumner saw an opportunity for the
Republican Party in this Reconstruction period. If the
Republican Party was outspoken in its support for giving
freed slaves the right to vote, then those new voters would
be more likely to vote Republican.

This struggle over who would decide how Reconstruction would be handled pitted leaders of Congress against the president. It was significant for the future of the Republican Party as well as for the future of the country. The weak Johnson, lacking support from other Republican Party members, would lose the battle and create a perception that the Republican Party was a "congressional party," a political party that favored a strong Congress at the expense of a weaker president. Supporters of this view argued that Congress more accurately reflected the will of the people, that congressmen—as representatives from different states—were true reflections of what the diverse population of the United States wanted.

There were numerous conflicts between Johnson and Congress. These differences resulted in a vote by the House of Representatives to impeach (remove from office) Johnson. Next came a trial in the Senate, where Johnson barely escaped conviction by one vote. He served the remaining months of Lincoln's term, continuing to veto congressional laws related to Reconstruction; however, Congress overrode his vetoes, and the plans of the so-called "Radical Republicans" for Reconstruction were passed.

GENERAL GRANT

Both the Democratic and Republican parties had wanted the victorious Union general Ulysses S. Grant to be their candidate for the presidency in 1868. Despite the fact that Grant was not a Republican, he agreed to be nominated by the Republican Party. The popular war hero was

Ulysses S. Grant *(above)* was able to parlay his success as Union general during the Civil War into victory as the Republican presidential candidate in 1868.

elected president. This marked the beginning of a real Republican dominance in national politics. The Democratic Party—identified with the defeated South—was seriously weakened, and Republicans would control the White

House for most of the seven decades that followed the election of Grant.

Grant soon surrounded himself with cabinet officials and advisers who were, for the most part, wealthy businessmen. This was the beginning of the connection between the Republican Party and big business. It was an era in which rapid development was taking place throughout the United States, with rights for things like forest development, mining, grazing, and farming being parceled out to the highest bidder. Today, many political candidates discuss conservation of natural resources as a part of their policies, but in the 1860s this concept did not exist. Instead, there was a belief in America as a land of limitless resources and a sense that progress depended on making sure that these resources were used.

Grant also believed that policymaking was an important function of Congress and that the president's role was to serve as more of an administrator. This, too, became a part of the Republican Party's philosophy of the time—a strong, activist Congress with a president who then made sure that the laws passed by Congress were carried out.

Grant was not a politician. He was a soldier. At a time when so many around him were scheming for power, he knew that he had been elected to office because he was a hero. During the campaign, voters were reminded to "vote the way you shot," a not-too-subtle reminder that the Civil War had been won by Grant and a vote against him (and the Republicans) would be a betrayal of the hard-won Union Army victory.

Scandals and corruption marked Grant's presidency, but Grant himself was never proved to be directly involved. He was nominated again for the presidency in 1872. Grant's scandal-ridden presidency and the harsh policies of some Republican leaders toward the Southern states during the Reconstruction period prompted a split in the Republican ranks, however. There were the "Radical Republicans," who believed that the South—as the defeated party in the Civil War—must immediately submit to all regulations dictated by the federal government, no matter what economic or social hardship they caused. There was also a new group of Republicans who favored a more moderate approach to Reconstruction and who strongly disapproved of the corruption that was a factor in the Grant administration. They named themselves "Liberal Republicans."

This split became evident in the presidential election of 1872, when the Liberal Republicans—along with a group of Democrats—announced that they would nominate their own candidate for the presidency to run against Grant. The Liberal Republicans nominated Horace Greeley, a prominent journalist and publisher of the *New York Tribune,* one of the most influential newspapers in the North. Greeley had been outspoken in his opposition to slavery, even criticizing President Lincoln for moving too slowly to abolish it altogether. He supported equality for freed slaves but believed that the harsh economic restrictions imposed on the South after the Civil War were making it impossible for the South to fully rejoin the United

States—which won him support among Southern and border states. Some criticized his personal behavior as eccentric, and when the Liberal Republicans announced him as their candidate for the presidency, supporters of Grant quickly labeled Greeley unstable and too excitable. He was soundly defeated in the election, winning only six states (all border or Southern states).

3

The Elephant and Other Symbols

In the years that followed the Civil War, certain issues would come to dominate Republican Party politics and would do so for several decades. These included how best to handle Reconstruction, questions of corruption, ideas about reforming the way in which government jobs were awarded, and tariffs on imported goods.

After Grant's reelection, the corruption and scandals that had troubled his administration in its first term continued. Grant had been a strong general but was a weak president, and his administration was known for rewarding his supporters with political positions and laws favorable to their businesses or states. Gradually, voters became disgusted with the corruption, and, in the election of 1874, the Republicans lost control of Congress.

From that election came a symbol with which the Republican Party has been identified ever since: the elephant. The symbol first appeared in a political cartoon by Thomas Nast, which was published by *Harper's Weekly* in 1874. In Nast's cartoon, a donkey disguised as a lion was shown trying to frighten a group of animals. One of these animals was an elephant. In the cartoon, the donkey symbolized newspapers that supported the Democrats, who had been running a series of editorials that argued against Ulysses S. Grant serving a third term as president. The frightened-looking elephant represented, in Nast's view, Republican voters, who were being frightened by the newspapers into abandoning President Grant. Nast's symbols—the crafty donkey and the timid elephant—were seized upon and used by other cartoonists who wanted to show the results of Democratic attacks against the Republicans.

The symbols, initially intended to be critical of both Democrats and Republicans, became closely identified with both political parties. Eventually, Republicans would proudly claim the elephant as their symbol—not the timid elephant of Nast's cartoons, but instead an elephant that represented strength, solid values, and intelligence.

A GOLDEN AGE

In 1876, the Republicans nominated the governor of Ohio, Rutherford B. Hayes, as their candidate for president. Hayes had been elected three times as governor and had

Thomas Nast's 1874 cartoon first popularized the donkey as a symbol of the Democratic Party and the elephant as a representation of the Republican Party. Nast continued to publish similar drawings in *Harper's Weekly,* such as the one above from 1879.

a reputation for honesty and for giving out government jobs based on experience rather than on connections or favors owed. Hayes quickly made it clear that, if elected, he would remove federal troops from the South and would work for reform of the civil service system (the system by which federal jobs were awarded). This served to reunite the Radical Republicans and the Liberal Republicans.

Hayes faced another governor in his quest for the presidency: New York governor Samuel Tilden, the Democratic candidate for the presidency. A wealthy lawyer who counted many railroad companies as his clients, Tilden had built a reputation for his willingness to battle corruption. The election of 1876 would become known in American history as one of the most disputed presidential elections ever held. Tilden narrowly won a majority of the popular vote, but questions remained. Double and conflicting returns of electoral votes were reported in Florida, Louisiana, South Carolina, and Oregon.

To settle the question of who actually had won the presidency, Congress appointed an electoral commission that consisted of five senators, five representatives, and five justices of the Supreme Court. Eight were Republicans; seven were Democrats. The commission ultimately voted along party lines and, on March 2, 1877, Rutherford B. Hayes was awarded all of the electoral votes that had been in question, giving him a one-vote electoral majority (185 to 184).

Despite the questionable way in which he won the presidency, Hayes kept his promises to end Reconstruction and reform the civil service. He served only one term.

Reconstruction policies and the awarding of government jobs continued to dominate politics after Hayes. James A. Garfield was nominated as the Republican candidate in 1880, with Chester Arthur as vice president. Arthur was criticized by many for his reputation for giving jobs to loyal Republicans; however, when Garfield was assassinated by Charles Guiteau (who had unsuccessfully tried to become U.S. ambassador to France) after only four months in office, Arthur vowed to continue the anticorruption stance Garfield had adopted.

Arthur became a surprise champion of civil service reform, supporting the passage of the Pendleton Act, which created a civil service with requirements based on merit rather than political party membership. It was also under Chester Arthur that the first general federal immigration law, which prevented immigrants who were paupers (without any means of support), criminals, or insane from entering the United States, was passed.

Arthur won the admiration of many for his firm stance on civil service reform, but he alienated many Republicans who had benefited from the more lenient system. He was the only president denied renomination by his own party.

MUGWUMPS AND REBELLION

For the election of 1884, the Republicans chose James G. Blaine of Maine as their presidential candidate, despite Chester Arthur's desire to seek another term in office. Blaine was the ultimate Washington insider: He had served in the House of Representatives for 13 years and in the Senate for 5. He had been Speaker of the House and secretary of state.

If Blaine was an insider, his opponent, Democrat Grover Cleveland, was definitely a Washington outsider. In fact, when he was nominated for the presidency, he had only been to Washington, D.C., once. A former mayor of Buffalo and governor of New York, Cleveland had earned a reputation for honesty and a commitment to fighting corruption.

THE GOP

The abbreviation GOP is often used to refer to the Republican Party. The term was first used in the 1870s as an abbreviation for Grand Old Party (even though the Democratic Party was far older) in an article in the *New York Herald.* One other reference from 1875 used the term "G.O.P." to mean "gallant old party."

When the use of the still-unpredictable motorcars became popular, the phrase was adapted to mean "get out and push." During the 1964 presidential campaign, the Republicans referred to themselves as the GO Party, and the Nixon administration tried to appeal to younger voters by using the abbreviation to mean "Generation of Peace."

By the late 1970s, the phrase had reverted to its original meaning. Today, GOP once again means "Grand Old Party."

Source: "The Republican Party—GOP History," www.gop.com.

For the Republicans, the election of 1884 represented a geographic shift. They had developed a successful pattern of nominating a presidential candidate from the Midwest and a vice-presidential candidate from the East. Lincoln and Grant were from Illinois; Hayes and Garfield were from Ohio. Blaine was from Maine; his vice-presidential nominee, John Logan, was a congressman from Illinois. The strategy was designed to win uncertain states— the northeastern states generally voted Republican and the Southern states generally voted Democratic, but the midwestern states and the state of New York were less committed to a single party. In the 1884 election, the Democrats also capitalized on this geographic strategy: Cleveland was from New York and his vice-presidential nominee was Thomas Hendricks, the former governor of Indiana.

The Republican platform was relatively specific in the 1884 campaign. It called for a federally-mandated eight-hour workday, the regulation of corporations, and support for ensuring civil and political rights for all citizens. The Democrats adopted a similar platform. With little difference between the platforms of the two parties, the focus shifted to the candidates themselves.

These two candidates would quickly become enmeshed in one of the nastiest political campaigns in American history. Questions were raised about the morals and past behavior of both Blaine and Cleveland. Gossip and rumors were published in leading newspapers.

Blaine had made enemies within his party, and a group of them, known as mugwumps, soon left the Republicans and began to campaign for Cleveland. Supporters of Blaine criticized these mugwumps for joining a party that one supporter controversially labeled as being linked to "Rum, Romanism [Catholicism] and Rebellion."

The election was very close—only 23,000 votes separated the two candidates. Cleveland, however, took New York, and with it won the presidency. It was the first defeat for the Republicans since Lincoln's election. After 24 continuous years in the White House, the Republicans were no longer leading the nation.

RECAPTURING THE WHITE HOUSE

The election of 1888 focused on the tariff laws on imported goods. Cleveland, running for reelection, favored changing them; the Republicans were opposed.

The Republicans nominated Benjamin Harrison of Indiana as their candidate, returning to the winning formula of a presidential candidate from the Midwest. Benjamin Harrison had a distinguished war record and notable ancestors: His great-grandfather, also named Benjamin Harrison, had been a signer of the Declaration of Independence; his grandfather, William Henry Harrison, was the ninth president of the United States.

It is interesting to note that, during this period in America's history, elections were often close, with results not being clear for some time. The election of 1888 was no

The Republicans nominated Benjamin Harrison *(above)* as their candidate in 1888. Although Harrison's presidency produced many notable achievements, the United States also experienced an economic downturn during that time, which led to Harrison's defeat when he ran for reelection in 1892.

exception. Once again, the Republicans lost the popular vote but won the presidency by capturing the necessary majority of electoral votes. This time, the Republicans also took New York. Perhaps more important, they simultaneously gained control of the White House and of Congress for the first time since 1875.

Harrison's presidency produced many notable achievements. He spoke out forcefully in favor of protecting and conserving America's forests. He had ambitious plans for foreign policy, including U.S. expansion in the Pacific and the construction of a canal that would cross Central America. He focused on expanding and modernizing the U.S. Navy and convened the first Pan-American Conference, cementing ties between the United States and Central America.

His record on civil rights is noteworthy for its time. He supported two bills that were designed to prevent Southern states from denying African Americans the right to vote. He appointed former slave Frederick Douglass as minister to Haiti.

Benjamin Harrison understood the connection between trade and foreign policy and negotiated several important trade agreements. It is in the area of trade and the economy, however, that he encountered the harshest criticism. Harrison supported Republican efforts to pass the landmark Sherman Anti-Trust Act, which was the first bill ever to attempt to limit the power of the large corporations in the United States: Harrison also favored high tariffs on imported goods, and, during his administration, the Republican-controlled Congress passed the McKinley Tariff Act. This act was designed to tax incoming goods at a high rate in order to encourage Americans to buy goods made in the United States. Suffering from a recession, American companies responded by raising the prices of their products.

The reaction from consumers was ultimately devastating to the Republican Party. In the congressional elections of 1890, the party was soundly defeated, and, when Harrison sought reelection in 1892, he lost to the man he had defeated four years earlier: former president Grover Cleveland.

SILVER AND GOLD

The economic downturn had caused Harrison's defeat, and it troubled Cleveland's second term in office, as well. The country slipped into a severe economic depression; many businesses closed during what became described as the Panic of 1893, a period when homelessness soared and nearly one-quarter of all working Americans lost their jobs. Cleveland served only one term.

The final election of the nineteenth century pitted Republican candidate William McKinley, the governor of Ohio, against William Jennings Bryan, a famous speaker with more progressive views on issues like regulating child labor and giving women the right to vote. McKinley's rise to the top of the ticket was in large part the work of Cleveland businessman Mark Hanna.

Hanna had progressive views on labor: He believed that there needed to be a greater emphasis on the responsibilities that both a company's management and its workers had to each other. He became a well-known figure in the field of employer-employee relations.

Hanna understood that the Republican Party had reached a crossroads. The philosophy that had inspired party loyalty immediately after the Civil War—"vote the way you shot"—was outdated. Americans were disgusted by the rise of very wealthy industrialists and wary of an economy that concentrated power in the hands of a select few. In Hanna's view, America could become a classless society, where all could benefit from its abundant resources. He believed that his state's governor—William McKinley—could become the president, and he set about to make this a reality. Hanna focused on wooing delegates in the South, in the Ohio Valley, and in the region of the Great Lakes.

At the Republican convention, held in St. Louis, an issue arose that would ultimately divide the party: whether the U.S. dollar should be backed by silver, which had become plentiful because of newly discovered silver mines in the West, or by gold (the then-current and more conservative approach). Under Hanna's guidance, the Republican convention initially avoided taking a position on the divisive issue in the party platform. Dissatisfied with the party's refusal to switch to the silver standard, a group of Republican delegates walked out on the convention. They formed their own party—the National Silver Party—and endorsed the Democratic candidate, Bryan, who supported the silver standard.

William McKinley *(above)* employed an unusual strategy in his campaign for the presidency: Instead of going out to meet people, he would invite voters to come to him, in a series of "front-porch meetings." The strategy was designed by Mark Hanna, who was then chairman of the RNC.

McKinley became the Republican nominee, and Hanna was chosen as the Republican National Committee's chairman. This marked a new era in the Republican Party—Hanna was not a chairman in name only, but a leader who devised the party's plans and mapped out its strategies. It was Hanna's idea that McKinley would spend his campaign for the presidency in his hometown of Canton, Ohio. Bryan was grabbing headlines by barnstorming (traveling) around the country, a revolutionary new tactic in campaigning. Hanna decided that the more reserved McKinley would not go out to meet the people—instead, he would bring the people to him, in a series of "front-porch meetings."

About 10 to 20 times a day, McKinley would walk out onto his front porch, dressed formally, and meet with different groups: editors, ministers, farmers, railroad workers, African Americans, and different religious groups. It was designed to emphasize McKinley's human side, as well as his refusal to make class distinctions—he welcomed all Americans to his front porch, the campaign suggested, and wanted to share his views with them.

Hanna revolutionized the Republican Party as he was masterminding the McKinley campaign. He opened two headquarters—one in Chicago and one in New York, although Chicago was the true center of activity. He centralized all national Republican activity through his office and installed a commercial bookkeeping and auditing system for the Republican Party, enabling him to control and oversee how money was being spent.

He professionalized the output of campaign literature, providing all of the major newspapers in the country with continuous information favorable to McKinley—carefully written and prepared to fit their newspapers' formats— and supplying them with articles and political cartoons. Millions of campaign leaflets were distributed from the New York and Chicago campaign headquarters.

Perhaps more important, Hanna also focused on fundraising in a way that had not previously been done by American political parties. In previous campaigns, the Republican Party normally ended an election cycle in debt. Hanna was determined to correct this and raised millions of dollars from wealthy industrialists and financiers.

Hanna pioneered the use of public opinion surveys, polling voters in critical states to determine the way in which they might vote. Once a state was determined to be safely in the camp of McKinley, Hanna could turn the focus to other states where voters were still undecided.

Hanna's hard work paid off. McKinley defeated Bryan, winning not only a large majority of the electoral votes (271 to 176) but also the popular vote. It was the first time in 25 years a Republican candidate had won a majority of the popular vote in a presidential election.

When the results were counted, it was clear that McKinley had won largely as a result of support from the business community and the industrial Northeast. Bryan's votes came largely from agricultural areas—the South, the West, and a large percentage of those in the working class. Many find this election significant because it marked the party loyalties that would shape both Republicans and Democrats into the twenty-first century. The Republicans were the party that supported business and industry and a conservative approach to economics.

4

A PROGRESSIVE
ERA

During McKinley's first term, the United States became more involved in world politics. There was a war with Spain—the 10-week Spanish-American War in 1898—and the United States added to its territory by acquiring Guam, Puerto Rico, and the Philippines, as well as by annexing (taking control of) Hawaii. In addition, McKinley's secretary of state called for an "open door" policy on trade with China.

America was emerging as a world power. Not all Republicans supported this new America, which seized territory and traded around the world. Some, mainly the older Republicans who had supported Lincoln from the days of the party's founding, opposed this idea of America as a colonial power. They remembered when the party had stood proudly on an antislavery platform and viewed the seizing of territories in the Pacific as a different form of slavery.

They were in the minority, though, and McKinley was the party's nominee in 1900. McKinley's vice president had died in office, and the Republican Party's new choice for vice president in 1900 was Theodore Roosevelt, the governor of New York. Roosevelt had earned a reputation as a war hero during the Spanish-American War. He was brash and outspoken, a leader and an organizer, and his placement on the ticket gave the Republicans appeal in the West and in other regions of the country where previously the Democrats had dominated.

William Jennings Bryan was once again the Democratic nominee, and again McKinley defeated him. Mark Hanna, who had been elected to the Senate in 1898, was McKinley's campaign manager and had brilliantly demonstrated to voters how prosperous the economy had become under McKinley by commissioning campaign posters depicting a full dinner pail.

McKinley was assassinated in 1901, shot during an appearance at the Pan-American Exposition in Buffalo, New York. He died on September 14, and Theodore Roosevelt was sworn in as president.

COWBOY REFORMER

His personal popularity had helped ensure Roosevelt a place on the Republican ticket, but during his time as president he would lead a series of economic, political,

Theodore Roosevelt *(above)* was vice president under
McKinley and assumed the office when McKinley was
assassinated in 1901. Roosevelt did not like Mark Hanna's
leadership of the RNC and set out to take control of
his party.

and social reforms that would transform the Republican Party platform. Roosevelt was intelligent, a great reader, and hardworking, as well as a master at the art of politics.

Roosevelt's first step upon becoming president was to assume control of the Republican Party. Roosevelt was determined that it would be he, not Mark Hanna, who directed the party. He placed men who were loyal to him in key positions and gradually used his connections and his office to transform the Republican Party into his party.

Conservation was a key issue for Roosevelt, and so it became a key issue for the Republican Party. Roosevelt proposed stricter regulation of businesses; when Congress seemed reluctant to pass legislation, Roosevelt took his case directly to the people. At times, Roosevelt clashed with others in his party on issues such as railroad regulation, government intervention in strikes, and the amounts that corporations could contribute to federal election campaigns. Nevertheless, he was reelected by a majority in 1904 and continued his efforts to promote conservation and regulate businesses.

For a brief period of time, under Roosevelt's leadership, the Republican Party moved from a conservative to a more progressive stance. He chose not to run for reelection in 1908, instead urging support for his friend, William Howard Taft of Ohio. Roosevelt had wanted to nominate Taft to the Supreme Court, but Taft had refused. He did finally allow Roosevelt to appoint him secretary of war and later put forward his name as a presidential candidate.

Taft campaigned on a Republican ticket that emphasized the party's wish to continue the policies begun by

Roosevelt—further regulation of businesses and revision of tariffs on imported goods. The connection to the popular Roosevelt helped ensure Taft's victory over William Jennings Bryan, the Democratic nominee for the third time. Taft soon ran into conflict with the more liberal members of the Republican Party, however, first over a failure to pass the promised tariff revisions and later in a conflict with the head of the Division of Forestry. This leader had been outspoken in his criticism of his supervisor, the secretary of the interior, and Taft was forced to fire him. The firing of a man appointed by Roosevelt led to rumors that Taft would reverse the steps Roosevelt had taken for conservation and sell natural resources to private corporations.

The result was a split in the Republican Party between those loyal to Taft and a more liberal group, led by Robert M. La Follette of Wisconsin, who organized the National Progressive Republican League in 1911. Their plan was to take control of the Republican Party away from the more conservative Republicans allied with Taft.

The split within the Republican Party was further deepened by a split between Taft and his former friend and supporter, Roosevelt. Roosevelt was displeased by some of the policies Taft was supporting and also by the men with whom Taft had surrounded himself.

At the Republican convention, held in Chicago in 1912, Roosevelt challenged Taft for the nomination. When it became clear that his bid would prove unsuccessful, Roosevelt announced that he viewed the Republican convention as unofficial. He left the party with his supporters and announced his intention to form a third party and to run for the presidency as that party's candidate.

Roosevelt's supporters swiftly began to attack the Republican Party, charging its leadership with trying to steal the election. The focus of this new, independent party would be on progress, and its name soon became the Progressive Party (it was also called the Bull Moose Party).

The Republican and Progressive parties' platforms showed similarities. They both favored limiting campaign funds, improving inland waterways, and conserving natural resources. The Progressive Party, however, called for a federal commission to regulate trusts, an easier method for amending the constitution, and the right for women to vote. The Progressives also focused on what they called "social and industrial justice"—calling for national and state laws to improve working conditions, make child labor illegal, and regulate workers' hours and pay.

Taft and Roosevelt were joined in the campaign by the Democratic nominee, Woodrow Wilson, the former president of Princeton University and governor of New Jersey. Three strong candidates, with strong public and party support, canvassed the country trying to appeal to voters. Roosevelt focused the bulk of his attacks not on Taft but on Wilson. In one campaign speech in Milwaukee, Roosevelt was actually shot while speaking and yet urged the crowd not to hurt the shooter, continuing to speak while waving a bloody handkerchief. The divided Republican Party provided Woodrow Wilson with a far easier path to the White House than he might have enjoyed had he faced a single candidate and a unified Republican organization.

A DIVIDED PARTY

As Wilson's first term in office drew to a close, leaders within the Republican and Progressive parties were determined to avoid another three-way race that would ensure Wilson a second term in office. As an effort to begin the negotiations, both the Republican and Progressive political conventions were scheduled for the same week in the same city—Chicago.

Roosevelt was an obstacle to unity once more. The Progressives wanted him to be their candidate; the Republicans were firmly opposed. They instead supported the candidacy of Charles Evan Hughes, a former governor of New York who was currently serving as a justice on the U.S. Supreme Court. Hughes was initially reluctant to be nominated, but friends pressured him to accept the call to seek the presidency. It would be the first time that a major political party had taken its presidential candidate from the Supreme Court. Hughes's running mate was Charles Fairbanks, who had served as vice president under Roosevelt.

The Progressive Party nominated Roosevelt, but he finally announced that he would not be a candidate for the presidency. Some disappointed Progressives reluctantly then cast their support to the Republican candidate, but many more left the party for good. The Republican Party succeeded in blocking Roosevelt from seeking office but failed to attract all of his faithful supporters.

It also failed at winning the presidency. A key element of Wilson's campaign was his pledge to keep the United States out of the war in Europe. He would win reelection but fail to keep his promise. The United States would be drawn into World War I, and Republicans would regain control of the House of Representatives and the Senate in 1918 elections. That Republican majority would vote against U.S. participation in the League of Nations, an organization that Wilson had championed. It was a bitter defeat for the wartime president.

VOTES FOR WOMEN

The election of 1920 was the first presidential election in which women could vote. Roosevelt had died in 1919, once and for all eliminating any effort to nominate him again for the presidency.

There was no clear frontrunner to represent the Republicans in 1920. Republican leaders had drawn up a list of qualifications that the ideal nominee would possess: He would have to have been someone who had opposed the League of Nations (to keep him consistent with the majority of the Republicans in the House and Senate), yet one who would be willing to see the United States eventually participate with certain reservations (to avoid alienating those Republicans who supported the League). He would have to have been a firm supporter of the Republican Party—anyone who had slipped away to join the Progressives in 1912 need not apply. He needed to be a man of the people,

The election of 1920 was the first presidential election in which women could vote, following the passage of the Nineteenth Amendment in August 1920. Before that, however, many women were voting in state elections, as these female New Yorkers did in 1917.

to appeal to a nation that wanted more accessible leaders. He would need to be willing to work with the powerful Republican-controlled Senate.

Few candidates could successfully meet all of these criteria, and finally the powerful Republican leadership turned to an unlikely candidate—the little-known Warren G. Harding, an Ohio senator whose major experience in the public eye had been his delivering of the nominating address for President Taft at the 1912 convention. Harding seemed willing to cooperate with the Republican leadership. His strongest supporter, Harry Daugherty of Ohio, urged his nomination because "he looked like a president."

When the convention seemed deadlocked, the intervention of a group of powerful Republican senators gave Harding the nomination. The Republican Party had drifted once more in the direction of a weaker presidency.

Harding and his vice-presidential nominee, Calvin Coolidge, won in a landslide over their Democratic opponent, James Cox. As with other weak presidents who owed much to influential supporters, though, the Harding administration would soon be hampered by scandal and charges of corruption.

Harding's major accomplishment was the creation of the Bureau of the Budget, the first formal office charged with preparing an annual budget for the federal government. It was also under Harding that large corporations began to merge, creating powerful companies that dominated in industry, finance, utilities, and transportation. Harding made several disastrous appointments, including naming an anticonservationist as secretary of the interior and not responding more strongly to corruption within his administration. Many of the actions taken by Republican administrations in the areas of conservation and eliminating trusts were halted during Harding's presidency.

The Republicans were spared facing a reelection campaign with charges of corruption and mismanagement against their candidate by the sudden death of Harding from a blood clot in his brain. His vice president, Calvin

Coolidge, made up for many of the blunders of his predecessor. The country was also enjoying a time of prosperity that helped cement the uncharismatic Coolidge's good fortune.

Coolidge was serious and solemn, but he seemed to symbolize an honesty and thriftiness that Americans liked in their president. As vice president, Coolidge had refused the use of a government car, instead driving his own Model-T Ford. Before becoming vice president, he had lived in a half-double (two-family) home in Massachusetts. He was shown baiting his fishing pole with worms rather than fancy lures.

As president, Coolidge took strict action against the members of the Harding administration charged with corruption. Through his handling of the scandal, he ensured that the Republican Party was not smeared in the process. Coolidge, however, also opposed the kinds of social-protection laws that might have shielded U.S. workers against the effects of the Great Depression that was in the not-too-distant future. He opposed unemployment insurance, supported dramatic reductions in taxes, and increased the tariffs on imported goods, poisoning trade with the many overseas customers for U.S. goods, who responded with high tariffs of their own—this time on American products.

Coolidge won reelection in 1924; when he chose not to run in 1928, the Republicans nominated Herbert Hoover, who had served in the cabinets of both Harding and Coolidge. Hoover had an outstanding reputation as an

Calvin Coolidge *(above)* was honest and thrifty, qualities that Americans liked in their president. He became president after Warren G. Harding died in office, then was elected in his own right in 1924.

engineer and humanitarian: He had served as director of a Belgian relief effort during World War I, leading a campaign to provide food to those trapped by the war. Hoover was not a politician, though: The presidency was his first experience in seeking elected office.

Hoover's campaign focused on continuing the economic prosperity that voters had enjoyed under Harding and Coolidge. The key slogan devised by the Republicans was "A Chicken in Every Pot." Hoover stated in his campaign that his focus would be on ensuring that poverty was "banished from this nation."

This campaign pledge of prosperity would prove disastrous for the Republican Party when the Great Depression swept over the country after Hoover took office. The steps taken by Hoover and his administration were unable to stop the collapse of the economy, and Hoover tried for too long to convince a desperate public that aid was a matter for local and private organizations, not the federal government, to provide.

Hoover was defeated in his bid for reelection by the Democratic candidate, Franklin D. Roosevelt of New York, in one of the largest landslides in U.S. history. Roosevelt attracted many long-time supporters of the Republican Party, including African Americans, who had always supported the party that first provided them with the right to vote.

For 70 years, the Republican Party had been a dominant player in national politics. That era had come to an end. Republicans would not regain the presidency for the next two decades.

5

REVIVING
THE PARTY

From 1932 to 1952, Republicans failed in their bids to capture the White House. Candidates like Alf Landon, Wendell Wilkie, and Thomas Dewey were no match for the overwhelming popularity of Franklin D. Roosevelt.

The Republican position on the war in Europe in the 1930s was isolationist: They supported efforts to keep the United States out of the war. After Japanese planes bombed Pearl Harbor and the United States entered World War II, however, Republicans rallied around the president in the war effort. Roosevelt ran for—and was elected to—four terms as president, but he died before completing his fourth term.

Roosevelt's successor, Harry S. Truman, was not as popular as Roosevelt. Still, Truman pulled a surprise

Many people predicted that Thomas Dewey would have an easy victory against Democratic candidate Harry S. Truman. Above, Truman holds the famous early edition of the *Chicago Daily Tribune*, which incorrectly stated that he had been defeated.

upset over New York governor Dewey at a time when polls had predicted a Dewey victory.

The Republicans had nominated Dewey to run against both Truman and Roosevelt, believing that Dewey's reputation as a reformer and a supporter of civil rights legislation in his home state of New York, and his efforts on behalf of education and health care while supporting a balanced budget, would appeal to voters. Under Franklin Roosevelt and his "New Deal" policies, the role of the federal government had expanded dramatically. Republicans had traditionally argued against this increased power for the federal government, but voters believed that the New Deal had brought an end to the Depression and provided many Americans with the jobs that they badly needed. Dewey's position was more moderate than that of some Republicans. He argued that many of the New Deal reforms were excessive, yet stated that there was a role for the federal government in helping to support the public interest.

Dewey had served as governor of New York, and he had won 46 percent of the popular vote against Roosevelt. Many predicted that he would have an easy victory against Truman. The pollsters were proved wrong, as captured in a famous photograph that shows the victorious Truman proudly bearing an early edition of the *Chicago Daily Tribune* with the incorrect headline, "DEWEY DEFEATS TRUMAN." In the final days before the election, Truman had chosen to ignore the press and the polls and go directly to the people in a "whistle-stop" campaign that rapidly took him from one city to another to speak directly to the voters. Despite having the support of only 15 percent of the nation's daily newspapers, Truman won the election.

A WAR HERO

After losing five presidential elections in a row, it was clear that the Republican Party needed to rethink its strategy. For too many years—under Harding, Coolidge, and Hoover in the most recent history—its campaign strategy had focused on a return to normalcy, keeping the nation on the same course that had previously brought it success in industrialization, trade, and expansion. That philosophy had collapsed with the Great Depression, and now it was the Democrats who could claim credit for the country's prosperity, for its success in World War II, and for the economy that had boomed during the war years. The Republican Party had become identified with defeat, with the Depression, and with conservative policies that some Democrats (including Truman) had successfully labeled as antilabor, antifarmer, anticonsumer, anticonservation, and anti- just about everything else.

The first step for the Republican Party lay in a dramatic rethinking of how to plan a political campaign. For too many years, the focus had been on winning geographic sections of the country—the East, the South, the Midwest, the West. At the turn of the century, large cities had always voted Republican, but this had shifted with the Depression. The Republicans needed to take a new kind of approach in the middle part of the twentieth century—an approach that targeted specific interest groups, rather than geographic regions. Republicans needed to find a way to appeal to farmers, laborers, urban voters, and younger voters.

The conflict became clear at the 1952 Republican convention. Senator Robert Taft of Ohio was the choice for president of many of the older, more experienced Republicans. Taft was conservative and no supporter of the New Deal, but he did support federal assistance in public housing and education. He had the support of a popular hero of World War II, General Douglas MacArthur, and had name recognition as the son of President William Howard Taft.

In making it clear that he would not again run for the presidency, Thomas Dewey had urged support for the commander of the Allied Forces in World War II, General Dwight D. Eisenhower, who was then serving as president of Columbia University. At the Republican convention, it became clear that Eisenhower also had the support of 23 of the 25 Republican governors, all of whom had had the experience of defeating a Democratic opponent and most of whom were considerably younger than the supporters of Taft. Political maneuvering eventually ensured the nomination of Eisenhower.

Eisenhower proved to be better at casual talks with voters than with prepared speeches or television appearances. He was plainspoken and direct, and he stood in sharp contrast to the more polished Democratic candidate, Illinois governor Adlai Stevenson. The widening conflict in Korea, involving American troops, was a boon to Eisenhower's candidacy, as he spoke confidently of his assessment of the status of the American military and how the conflict should be handled. Eisenhower expressed a certainty that he could end the war and promised to go to Korea if elected to bring the war to an end.

Eisenhower triumphed in a landslide, winning 39 of the 48 states then in the United States (Alaska and Hawaii were not admitted until 1959) and 442 electoral votes to Stevenson's 89. The Eisenhower victory decisively brought

General Dwight D. Eisenhower was celebrated for his military victories during World War II. He spoke with American paratroopers in England in 1944 *(above)*. These victories bolstered his candidacy for president in 1952.

an end to two decades of Democratic domination of the White House. It was more an Eisenhower victory than a Republican one, however: Eisenhower's personal charm, winning smile, direct talk, and confidence had appealed to the nation.

MODERN REPUBLICANISM

Eisenhower was in many ways new to the game of politics when he began his presidency. His overwhelming victory made him the clear head of the Republican Party, and he set about rebuilding that party in a new form, a form that he would eventually label "Modern Republicanism."

The Modern Republicans would no longer campaign against the New Deal—in fact, Republicans would even attempt to expand some of the social and economic reforms launched under Franklin Roosevelt. The U.S. economy would depend on private enterprise, and the government would ensure that the economy remained stable and continued to grow. These were the philosophies that Modern Republicanism needed to embrace, according to Eisenhower. Eisenhower also believed that Modern Republicanism should stand for the elimination of discrimination based on race and religion, ignoring the fact that many supporters of segregation (especially in the South) had voted for him because they opposed Truman's policy of integrating the military.

These issues of Modern Republicanism were certain to appeal to voters. In addition, they were issues that the Democrats had difficulty criticizing because many of them were, in fact, issues traditionally identified with the Democratic Party.

In the 1956 election, Eisenhower once again faced Adlai Stevenson. Eisenhower was overwhelmingly popular—so popular that Stevenson only alienated voters when he attacked Eisenhower personally. Eisenhower had had a heart attack and an intestinal operation before the conventions. In one ad, the Stevenson campaign attacked Eisenhower's less popular vice president, Richard Nixon, asking voters if they were comfortable with a "President

Richard Nixon"—a hint at questions about whether Eisenhower's health could permit him another term in office.

Eisenhower's campaign for reelection was extremely successful. In the midst of the Cold War—the conflict between
the Soviet Union and the United States—Eisenhower had
dedicated himself to peace while ensuring that the United
States took its place as a world power. It was Eisenhower

CIVIL RIGHTS ACTS OF 1957

In 1957, Congress passed the Civil Rights Act of 1957. This
created a civil-rights division within the Department of Justice. This division was charged with investigating cases that
involved a violation of an individual's or group's civil rights and
enforcing civil-rights laws throughout the nation.

At its beginning, the division was very small; fewer than
10 lawyers worked on civil-rights cases. This small group
quickly began to investigate claims of voting-rights violations
in the South. The division has expanded considerably over
the years, and today more than 350 lawyers help to enforce
civil-rights law.

The Civil Rights Act of 1957 failed to dramatically increase
the number of African Americans registered to vote, and it did
not offer adequate protection to those who did wish to cast a
ballot. The conflict would continue over several years, raising
questions about the extent to which the federal government
should interfere with voting policies and practices of the individual states in order to protect the rights of its citizens.

who created the image of the Republican Party as a party of peace.

The result was another overwhelming victory and an endorsement of the principles of Modern Republicanism. For several decades, the Democratic Party had been the party of most Americans, and Eisenhower was determined to change that.

It is important to note that Modern Republicanism was still essentially a conservative platform. Taxes on the wealthy were lowered. In foreign affairs, specifically in the Cold War, the Republicans favored a strong anti-Communist position, designed to prevent other countries from falling under the influence of the Soviet Union.

Civil rights became a key issue during Eisenhower's presidency. Eisenhower signed the Civil Rights Acts of 1957 and 1960, and he sent federal troops to Arkansas in 1957 to enforce court-ordered racial integration of a high school. In the elections, support for the Republicans came from business owners and the growing number of middle-class voters moving to the suburbs.

Eisenhower's vice president, Richard Nixon of California, failed to win the election of 1960. Nixon had reached out to different wings within the Republican Party, attempting to unify the party behind him as its candidate. One of the issues that Nixon campaigned on was a commitment to civil rights. When civil-rights leader Martin Luther King Jr. was sentenced to four months of hard labor in a Georgia prison, however, neither President Eisenhower nor Nixon acted to secure his

Television was just beginning to become a factor in political campaigns in 1960, when Democrat John F. Kennedy *(left)* and Republican Richard Nixon *(right)* ran against each other. The handsome, young Kennedy benefited from this and won the presidency that year.

release. Instead, it was the Democratic nominee, Senator John F. Kennedy, who called Mrs. King and offered his assistance.

Television was just beginning to become a factor in political campaigns in 1960. Kennedy benefited from this: He was young and handsome, appearing far more relaxed and confident on television than Nixon.

Nixon also struggled with the Republican leadership. He had faced a strong challenge for the nomination from the governor of New York, Nelson Rockefeller. He insisted on micromanaging the campaign, refusing to delegate and often appearing indecisive. For the presidential election, he had pledged to campaign in all 50 states and did so, leaving his opponent to concentrate on certain key states with more electoral votes at stake.

It was a close election, despite the advantages Kennedy enjoyed. Nixon benefited from Eisenhower's endorsement and popularity. Republicans, outnumbered three to two by Democratic voters, demonstrated greater party loyalty, and the voter turnout—62.7 percent of those eligible to vote—was extraordinarily high. In the end, though, the Democratic ticket proved successful and Richard Nixon was defeated.

6

A MORE CONSERVATIVE GOP

At the time of the 1964 convention, the Republican Party was in chaos. President Kennedy had been assassinated, and his successor, Texan Lyndon B. Johnson, was running as the Democratic candidate. Two factions within the Republican Party—the moderates and the conservatives—were in conflict over the future of the party.

The conservatives ultimately triumphed, arguing that a conservative philosophy was key to winning the election. The Republicans nominated Barry Goldwater, a senator from Arizona, but not without a fight in which other Republicans suggested that Goldwater was too extreme.

He was an outspoken critic of Republican policies that seemed too much like those of the Democrats and even labeled the Eisenhower administration "a dime store New Deal." Although he helped to end segregation in schools in Phoenix, Arizona, and in the Arizona National Guard, he voted against the Civil Rights Act of 1964 and was criticized for apparently supporting the use of nuclear weapons in war.

The convention brought these divisions within the Republican Party into the open. When Nelson Rockefeller stood up to address the convention, supporters of Goldwater drowned him out with loud boos. Goldwater had been drafted by conservatives within the Republican Party who had once supported Taft in his challenge to Eisenhower. They were dissatisfied with the policies of the Eisenhower years and felt that Nixon's defeat in 1960 had proved that those policies would not win elections.

Goldwater did not win the election, but his campaign marked an important beginning for the Republican Party: the rise of a strong conservative movement within the Republican ranks. Goldwater represented a power shift away from more liberal Republicans, often described as "Eastern." By the mid-1960s, the country was undergoing a tremendous transformation. Geographically, power—at least in terms of population and economic growth—was shifting away from traditional places like New York and to new areas like the so-called Sunbelt, where cities like Los Angeles, Dallas, and Houston were becoming more powerful and important. The Midwest,

Believing that a more conservative candidate was the answer to the chaotic political situation of the 1960s, Republicans nominated Barry Goldwater as their presidential candidate in 1964. Above, Goldwater greets supporters during a campaign stop in Illinois.

South, and Southwest were becoming important centers of Republican influence. Goldwater appealed to voters in these new regions, who were generally more conservative than those on the East Coast.

Goldwater attracted Southern voters to the Republican Party—voters who were opposed to the civil-rights movement. Goldwater stated that he was opposed to racism, but he supported the rights of individual states and argued that federal efforts to intervene in desegregation were unconstitutional. Goldwater's foreign-policy platform was based on an effort to achieve victory over Communism, and he was strongly opposed to any efforts to disarm the United States. The Republicans chose Goldwater in part out of a belief that previous elections had been lost not because there were more Democratic than Republican voters, but because conservative Republicans had not been given a strong candidate in the elections.

Goldwater had many liabilities. He was frank and outspoken, often offering opinions without thinking them through or considering how they might be reported in the media. He stuck to his positions, even when they proved unpopular. He criticized President Johnson's social programs—which he said created a "welfare state"—and instead offered an emphasis on traditional values, individual responsibility, self-reliance, and law and order. Goldwater would not win the presidency, but the conservative values that represented the Republican platform in 1964 would not be forgotten. They would become the key platform for the Republican Party nearly 20 years later and would propel the Republican governor of California—Ronald Reagan, an outspoken supporter of Goldwater in 1964—to the presidency.

THE NIXON YEARS

The election of 1968 came at a time of great unrest and uncertainty in the United States. Under President Lyndon Johnson, the number of Americans fighting in the war in Vietnam had increased from 16,000 in 1963 to more than 500,000. An antiwar movement was growing, accompanied by student protests at colleges and universities across the country. In April, Martin Luther King Jr. was assassinated, and riots in more than 100 cities followed his death. In June, Robert Kennedy, a Democratic candidate for president, was assassinated after winning the California primary.

The spectacle of disorder and violence under Democratic leadership was further emphasized by images from the Democratic convention itself. Held in Chicago, the convention included actual fights and shouting from supporters of the various candidates and violence between antiwar protestors and police in the streets. President Johnson had initially been the choice for the Democratic nomination, but he announced that he would not run after a disappointing result in the early primaries. Robert Kennedy had been a leading candidate, and after his assassination the last-minute nomination of Johnson's vice president, Hubert Humphrey, left a feeling of uncertainty and confusion within the Democratic Party.

The Republicans had nominated Richard Nixon; his choice for his running mate was Maryland governor Spiro Agnew. Confusion over the nomination and divisions over the U.S. involvement in the Vietnam War doomed Humphrey's campaign. Some Southern Democrats left their party altogether and voted for Governor George Wallace of Alabama, who ran on an anti-integration platform.

The Republican platform presented Nixon as a candidate who was strongly in favor of law and order; commercials featured Nixon's promise to bring an honorable end to the war in Vietnam. Nixon won the election, earning 301 electoral votes. The election marked the final end to the idea of the "Democratic South," with Republicans winning victory in 11 states there.

The Vietnam War soon became an issue that haunted the Republicans, however, particularly by the time Richard Nixon sought reelection. His 1968 campaign promise to end the war had not been kept; in fact, American involvement in the conflict had escalated. Inflation and unemployment were rising. Sensing that the election was slipping away, Nixon created a series of actions designed to add new prestige to his administration: He made diplomatic tours of Russia and China and ended the military draft—a move designed to appeal to younger voters, as the voting age had recently been lowered from 21 to 18.

Nixon's opponent, George McGovern, called for a complete withdrawal of American troops from Vietnam and a reduction in military spending. Despite evidence of a connection between a break-in at the Democratic National Committee headquarters at the Watergate complex and the Nixon administration, McGovern failed to convince voters. Nixon won reelection in a landslide.

Evidence of a connection between the White House and the break-in—and an attempt by Nixon to cover it up—would eventually force the president to resign. He was succeeded in the presidency by his vice president, Gerald Ford (his first vice president, Spiro Agnew, had been forced to resign earlier after being convicted of failure to pay his income taxes). The Watergate scandal, and the conviction of many members of the Nixon administration involved in it, caused a massive loss of confidence in elected officials and the government. Ford pardoned Nixon in an effort to spare the country the spectacle of a former president on trial, but the decision probably cost him the presidency when he ran again in 1976. In an election year during which character and integrity were principal concerns for voters, the Republican Party was hopelessly connected to the scandals of the Nixon White House. Ford was defeated by Georgia governor Jimmy Carter, whose campaign focused on his honesty, his roots as a simple Georgia peanut farmer, and what he represented as a Washington outsider.

MORNING IN AMERICA

In the 1976 election, Ford had faced a challenge from within his own party—Ronald Reagan, the conservative who had publicly supported Barry Goldwater several years earlier. Reagan failed to win the nomination but impressed many within the Republican Party. Four years later, many voters believed that the time was right for a more conservative approach to government. Under Carter, the United States was suffering from a poor economy, gas shortages, and a weakened image throughout the world. Also, a group of Iranians had seized hostages at the American embassy and held many of the 66 men and women for more than a year. A rescue attempt ended in humiliating failure.

The conservative ideals that Ronald Reagan offered to the Republican Party assured him the nomination and ultimately brought him the presidency. The Republican platform focused on increasing economic growth, restoring America's military strength and confidence, and standing up to the Soviet Union. Reagan spoke of America as a great nation, and his optimism and confidence represented a welcome shift away from the failures and battered economy of the previous four years.

Reagan won an overwhelming victory over Jimmy Carter; he received 489 electoral votes (Carter won 49) and 51 percent of the popular vote. Republicans also gained 12 additional seats in the U.S. Senate. For the first time in 25 years, Republicans held a majority in the Senate.

Witnessing the appeal of Reagan's conservative platform to voters, the Republican Party was willing to follow suit and adopt the more conservative policies that seemed to be what Americans wanted in the 1980s. Amidst concerns about the threat of the Soviet Union, Reagan launched a massive buildup of U.S. military forces, stating that he wanted peace but believing that "peace through strength" was the best way to achieve it. Reagan also introduced deep tax cuts, which led to an economic recovery.

Reagan was labeled the "Great Communicator" for his ability to connect with Americans. As a former actor, he was a master of the skills needed to convey his deeply held political beliefs—beliefs that had remained largely consistent for the past 20 years. His appeal was so great that many Democrats crossed party lines to vote Republican, giving rise to the term *Reagan Democrats*.

Reagan ran for reelection in 1984 against Jimmy Carter's vice president, Walter Mondale. The Democratic Party had chosen a woman, Representative Geraldine Ferraro of New York, as its vice-presidential candidate, but the

After the problematic Carter presidency, Ronald Reagan
(right) was seen by many people as the answer to America's
ills. In 1980, he challenged the incumbent Carter and won in
an overwhelming victory.

Mondale-Ferraro ticket was no match for Reagan's popularity or the success of the Republican Party's conservative message. Republican campaign ads proudly announced that it was "morning in America," showing images of a newly hopeful country in which the economy was in an upswing and oil prices were low. Reagan won an astonishing 59 percent of the popular vote and 525 electoral votes (to Mondale's 13). Republicans did lose

THE GREAT COMMUNICATOR

Ronald Reagan ushered in a new era, one in which conservative values became the values of the Republican Party, as outlined in his inaugural address:

> . . . We have every right to dream heroic dreams. Those who say that we're in a time when there are not heroes, they just don't know where to look. You can see heroes every day going in and out of factory gates. Others, a handful in number, produce enough food to feed all of us and then the world beyond. You meet heroes across a counter, and they're on both sides of that counter. There are entrepreneurs with faith in themselves and faith in an idea who create new jobs, new wealth, and opportunity. They're individuals and families whose taxes support the government and whose voluntary gifts support church, charity, culture, art, and education. Their patriotism is quiet, but deep. Their values sustain our national life. . . .

two Senate seats but still retained the majority, and the Democrats maintained control of the House.

Reagan had built a legacy in a Republican Party that now proclaimed its conservative policies while criticizing the "liberal, tax-and-spend" Democrats. The Republicans could proudly review their triumphs as Reagan became the first president since Eisenhower to serve two full terms.

In 1988, the Republicans turned to Reagan's vice president, George H.W. Bush, to carry on the Reagan legacy.

To those neighbors and allies who share our freedom, we will strengthen our historic ties and assure them of our support and firm commitment. We will match loyalty with loyalty. We will strive for mutually beneficial relations. We will not use our friendship to impose on their sovereignty, for our own sovereignty is not for sale.

As for the enemies of freedom, those who are potential adversaries, they will be reminded that peace is the highest aspiration of the American people. We will negotiate for it, sacrifice for it; we will not surrender for it, now or ever. . . .

Source: Ronald Reagan, "Inaugural Address, January 20, 1981," in *Conservatism in American Since 1930,* edited by Gregory L. Schneider. New York: New York University Press, 2003, pp. 344–345.

Bush had his own very impressive resume: In addition to serving as vice president, he had flown as a combat pilot in World War II, served as a congressman, and been ambassador to the United Nations, chairman of the Republican Party, and director of the Central Intelligence Agency.

The Reagan legacy proved to be a mixed blessing. The dramatic tax cuts and military buildup under Reagan had created a soaring federal deficit. Questions were raised about the Reagan administration's involvement in illegal sales of weapons to Iran and funding of a group of rebels in Nicaragua. The stock market had collapsed in 1987, and there were many news reports of insider-trading scandals.

The contest between George H.W. Bush and his Democratic challenger, Massachusetts governor Michael Dukakis, made 1988 a particularly bitter election year. The Republicans were able to portray Dukakis as a typical liberal, one who would increase government spending to fund the programs he proposed and weaken America militarily. Television ads suggested that, if elected, Dukakis would let convicted murderers out of prison. The Democrats were never able to mount an effective defense, and George H.W. Bush won the election, carrying 40 states and winning 54 percent of the popular vote. It was the first time in 60 years that a president was able to turn over the presidency to a successor from his own party.

TRANSFORMING WORLD

During President George H.W. Bush's four years in office, the United States witnessed several critical changes in

Reagan's vice president, George H.W. Bush *(right)*, ran for president in 1988, with Dan Quayle *(left)* as his running mate. While Bush was a very popular president, his campaign for reelection failed to recognize the worsening American economy, which helped Democrat Bill Clinton win the election.

foreign policy. The Soviet Union, which for many years had been one of the two superpowers in the world (the other being the United States), began to crumble. The influence of communism fell in Eastern Europe, most notably with the tearing down of the wall in Berlin that had once divided Germany into two nations. Republicans were quick to credit the tough policies advocated by Ronald Reagan as partially responsible. In 1990, under the direction of Saddam Hussein, Iraq invaded Kuwait. President Bush organized an international coalition to respond, bringing about a swift and decisive victory in what came to be known as the Persian Gulf War.

In 1991, after the decisive military victory in the war, President Bush's popularity was so high (near 90 percent of all Americans approved of his actions) that few Democrats were willing to challenge him in a presidential contest, one that seemed sure to prove victorious for the Republicans. Many leading Democrats decided not to run, and so the Democratic nomination was given to the little-known governor of Arkansas, Bill Clinton.

The Republicans, perhaps overly confident of victory after three successive presidential wins, failed to note the impact of a worsening economy, marked by rising prices and unemployment, on voters. The Democrats did not make this mistake. With the Soviet Union no longer a threatening superpower, the traditional conservative Republican message of a strong military failed to resonate with voters. What did resonate was the Democratic focus on the economy. Texas billionaire H. Ross Perot entered the campaign as an independent candidate, and his focus on deficit reduction underscored the economy as a central issue of the campaign. In addition, Perot appealed more to Republicans than to Democrats, pulling votes away from President Bush.

The comparison of Clinton's tough childhood—he grew up with an alcoholic stepfather—with Bush's life of privilege did not help the Republican cause. The Republican Party suddenly seemed to be out of touch with the struggles of average Americans—a party of the wealthy at a time when many Americans were out of work. The Democrats won 370 electoral votes to the Republicans'

160 (Perot did not win any states and so failed to win any electoral votes) and captured majorities in both the House of Representatives and the Senate. The president whose approval rating had once been 90 percent received only 37.5 percent of the popular vote. After 18 years of Republican leadership, the White House was now in Democratic hands.

7

THE REPUBLICAN PARTY TODAY

The Republican Party losses in 1992 can be attributed in part to the Democratic Party's success in claiming many of the issues that had traditionally been identified with Republicans. Presidential candidate Bill Clinton was a leader in this effort. He was described as a "new Democrat," one who moved away from the traditional liberal positions that favored a large government with an expanded role in social programs. Instead, Clinton spoke of ending the welfare system as it traditionally existed, encouraging its recipients to return to work, and focused on helping America build a strong economy.

Republican Party leaders in Congress were successful at blocking much of the legislation President Clinton

After Democrat Bill Clinton's election as president in 1992, key members of the Republican Party, including Newt Gingrich *(above)* signed a "Contract with America" in an attempt to revitalize the GOP.

had set as his top priorities at the beginning of the administration. By 1994, as midterm Congressional elections drew near, Republicans in Congress were determined to regain control of both the Senate and the House of Representatives.

Their plan involved creating a new political agenda for the Republican Party, one that could challenge the new direction that Clinton had set for the Democratic Party. The heart of this Republican agenda was drawn up by Georgia Congressman Newt Gingrich in a series of points he labeled a "Contract with America." Using information from polls and focus groups, Gingrich and the Republicans drafted a set of critical points that cleverly linked votes for Republicans running in local congressional races to an overall national program.

On September 27, 1994, 367 Republican candidates stood on the steps of the U.S. Capitol and staged a mass signing of the Contract with America, telling Americans that if they broke the promises of this contract, they should be removed from office. The three key principles of the contract—a reflection of Republican concerns—were accountability (the government is too big and spends too much, and elected officials have become unresponsive), responsibility (there needs to be a proper balance between government and personal responsibility), and opportunity (government regulations and harsh tax laws have made the American dream harder to achieve).

The contract also pledged that, within the first 100 days of assuming office, the members of Congress who signed the document would bring to the House floor the following bills:

1. The Fiscal Responsibility Act: an act to provide a balanced budget and tax-limit legislation for Congress.

2. The Taking Back Our Streets Act: an anticrime act.

3. The Personal Responsibility Act: an act to ban welfare to underage mothers and deny increased aid for mothers who had additional children while on welfare.

4. The Family Reinforcement Act: an act to provide enforcement for child support, tax incentives for adoption, and tax credits for those who cared for an elderly parent.

5. The American Dream Restoration Act: an act to offer a tax credit of $500 for each child, and other forms of middle-class tax relief.

6. The National Security Restoration Act: an act to ban the use of U.S. troops under command of the United Nations.

7. The Senior Citizens' Fairness Act: an act to raise the Social Security earnings limit and repeal a tax hike on Social Security benefits.

8. The Job Creation and Wage Enhancement Act: an act to offer incentives to small businesses and other programs to create jobs and raise worker pay.

9. The Common Sense Legal Reform Act: an act to impose limits on damages awarded in lawsuits and reform of product liability laws.

10. The Citizen Legislature Act: an act to limit the number of terms a congressman could serve.

The Contract with America was a brilliant strategy that proved extremely successful. Republicans were elected in record numbers, taking control of both the Senate and the House of Representatives for the first time since 1954. The author of the Contract with America, Newt Gingrich, was elected Speaker of the House. Republicans would maintain control of both houses of Congress for the remainder of Bill Clinton's presidency.

With such a clear mandate from voters, the Republicans in Congress quickly initiated efforts to pass the legislation designed to transform the country's welfare system and reduce the budget deficit. Their efforts were frequently confrontational toward Democrats, the president in particular, resulting in an impasse over the budget in late 1995 and early 1996 that in turn resulted in two partial shutdowns of the government.

A POLITICAL COMEBACK

The Republicans had viewed their legislative victory in 1994 as evidence that they could reclaim the presidency in 1996. The Democrats, however, were successful at depicting the Republicans as extremist and at fault for the two shutdowns of the government. Clinton also benefited from a strong economy and an absence of foreign policy crises.

In his campaign for reelection, Clinton proposed a number of laws designed to appeal to the majority of American voters—such as the Family Leave Act, which ensured that workers could take time off to care for a sick relative or a newborn baby without fear of losing their jobs; a college tuition act; and a ratings system for television programs. The Republican candidate, Kansas senator Robert Dole, was a respected figure who had a strong history of public service but failed to connect with voters. The Republican message focused on the scandals connected to the Clinton White House, but, at a time of prosperity, the Republican focus on character did not resonate with the American public. Clinton won a majority of the electoral and popular votes, although the Republicans did retain their control of Congress.

The relationship between conservative Republicans and Bill Clinton became increasingly hostile in the second term of his presidency. In 1998, an investigation into

President Clinton's involvement in a series of real estate and financial transactions while he was governor of Arkansas unearthed evidence of an inappropriate relationship between the president and a White House intern. In December 1998, the Republican majority in the House of Representatives voted to impeach Clinton. After a vote to impeach a president, a trial is held in the Senate. In this Senate trial, a group of more moderate Republicans joined with Democrats in voting to acquit the president. The impeachment trial divided the country; many Americans blamed the Republicans for putting the president on trial, viewing their actions as politically motivated.

COMPASSIONATE CONSERVATIVE

In the summer of 2000, the Republican National Convention nominated the governor of Texas, George W. Bush, as its candidate for president. Bush was the son of President George H.W. Bush. Many of the advisers and high-ranking officials in his father's administration were visible in the younger Bush's campaign, including the vice-presidential nominee, Richard (Dick) Cheney, George H.W. Bush's secretary of defense. The Democratic candidate was Bill Clinton's vice president, Al Gore.

The campaigns largely focused on the economy and on domestic matters. The Republicans and Democrats both focused on a few key issues: education, the future of Social Security, prescription drug plans for senior citizens, and the economy. Both Republicans and Democrats positioned themselves at the center. President George H.W. Bush had once proudly claimed his conservative connection with Ronald Reagan, but his son described himself as a compassionate conservative, one who focused on issues that directly affected ordinary Americans.

The Republicans hinted indirectly at the scandals that had involved the Clinton administration. Bush described himself as someone who would bring dignity back to the Oval Office.

The division over the handling of the Clinton impeachment trial was reflected in a sharply divided election—the closest in history. Because of disputed election results, the winner was not determined for 36 days after the election, and then resolution came only after a series of legal battles and a Supreme Court ruling. In the end, amid great controversy, the election was awarded to George Bush, his victory apparently having been determined by a bare 537 votes cast in Florida.

The Republicans also won a majority in both the House of Representatives and the Senate; however, when Republican Senator Jim Jeffords of Vermont announced his decision to become an independent in 2001, the Democratic Party became the majority party in the Senate.

The attacks on the United States on September 11, 2001, served to rally the country around President Bush. Approval of his handling of the crisis resulted in Republican victories in the midterm elections in 2002, in which Republicans recaptured the Senate and gained additional seats in the House of Representatives.

President Bush's decision to invade Iraq in March 2003 proved far less popular than his decision to invade Afghanistan after the September 11, 2001, attacks. The war was a central issue in the 2004 election campaign, in which President Bush was challenged by Democratic senator John Kerry of Massachusetts.

In the campaign, both the Republican and Democratic parties returned to the political strategy that had marked their parties during the Cold War. The Republicans emphasized that the world was an uncertain and threatening place, in which Americans needed the steady leadership that President Bush had provided as commander in chief. The Democratic ads painted Republicans as out of touch and emphasized John Kerry as more responsive to the needs of the typical voter.

The election was a close one. In the end, President Bush captured 274 electoral votes to John Kerry's 252.

THE REPUBLICAN PARTY TODAY

Although the leadership of the Republican Party has changed, certain key issues have become core defining issues for the Republican Party. In the earliest days of the Republican Party, an issue that marked Republicans was their unwillingness to accept the right of states to practice slavery. Today, the modern Republican Party is known for its policies that limit federal government and give greater powers to states and local governments in matters such as education.

Republican president George W. Bush, accompanied by Secretary of State Condoleezza Rice, gestures during a meeting with Iraq Provincial Reconstruction Team Leaders in March 2007.

It is difficult to define a typical Republican. Some Republicans support the death penalty; others oppose it. Some support a constitutional amendment to ban abortion; other Republicans define themselves as pro-choice.

There are, however, certain broad issues that are typical of the Republican Party. Republicans believe in reducing taxes, both to spark economic growth and to provide people with greater financial freedom. They oppose government regulation of the economy and excessive government-funded social programs. Most Republicans strongly oppose efforts to regulate gun ownership. In social issues, Republicans tend to be more conservative, particularly when it comes to issues such as prayer in schools and same-sex marriage.

In the area of foreign policy, Republicans favor strong national defense. In recent years, the Republican Party has also supported strong efforts to protect American security interests, whether within the U.S. borders or overseas.

Every four years, the Republican Party gathers at a national convention (held during the summer) to determine what its political platform will be and to nominate its presidential candidate. Delegates to the convention are selected during the winter and spring before the convention is held. Typically about 2,000 delegates attend the Republican National Convention. The Republican and Democratic conventions are not held at the same time; according to tradition, the current president's party holds its convention second.

Delegates to the Republican convention are chosen by primary elections in more than 40 states; other states hold caucuses to select their delegates. The Republicans follow a winner-take-all system for their delegates: The candidate who wins the most delegates in a state is awarded all of that state's delegates. This is different from the Democratic Party system, in which Democratic primaries give delegates in proportion, based on the number of votes a candidate receives (for example, Candidate A might receive 25 percent of the delegates, Candidate B might receive 20 percent, etc.). Because of this, Republicans tend to choose their presidential nominees more quickly than Democrats do.

The Republican Party is governed by a national committee that is chosen at the national convention for the following four-year period. This Republican National

Committee is made up of approximately 150 leaders who represent all of the states and territories in the United States. Usually the presidential nominee names the chairman of the Republican National Committee;

PLATFORM OF THE REPUBLICAN PARTY

In the 2004 presidential campaign, the Republican Party platform, titled "A Safer World and a More Hopeful America," claimed the following as its core issues:

Winning the War on Terror . . .
because our government's most solemn duty is keeping its citizens safe.
Ushering in an Ownership Era . . .
because a vibrant entrepreneurial spirit will keep our economy strong and provide more opportunities for workers and families.
Building an Innovative Economy to Compete in the World . . .
because America can compete with anyone, anywhere, thanks to our entrepreneurs and risk-takers who keep us on the cutting edge of technology and commerce.
Strengthening Our Communities . . .
because our children deserve to grow up in an America where all their hopes and dreams can come true.
Protecting Our Families . . .
because we respect the family's role as a touchstone of stability and strength in an ever-changing world.

Source: www.gop.com.

often it is someone who has helped that nominee during his campaign.

In 2004, the Republican Party platform carried the label "A Safer World and a More Hopeful America." The platform began with a tribute to Ronald Reagan, who had died earlier that year and yet continued to influence the party that he had helped to shape in a stronger and more conservative image. It continued with a reference to the first Republican president, Abraham Lincoln, describing him as one of the party's "greatest heroes." The major issues outlined in the platform were very different issues from those that the Republican Party first claimed at its founding, however: winning the war on terror, ushering in an ownership era, building an innovative economy, strengthening communities, and protecting families.

The party of Lincoln has evolved over the century and a half that it has existed. It has succeeded where other parties failed by redefining itself with each new generation to reflect the reality of life in America.

GLOSSARY

border states States that permitted slavery but did not leave the Union in 1860–1861; they included Delaware, Maryland, Kentucky, and Missouri.

civil service Government workers; employees of the government who are not elected officials and not members of the military.

Communism A political movement designed to use revolutionary methods to achieve a classless society in which all goods and property are owned by the society rather than by the individual.

conservation Preserving and protecting natural resources.

conservative Someone who wishes to limit change and to preserve traditional institutions and existing conditions.

convention A meeting of delegates to nominate a candidate for office and to make decisions about the policies and goals of a political party.

Copperhead A critical term used to describe Democrats who supported a negotiated settlement with the South at the time of the Civil War.

deadlock A stalemate, in which agreement or progress is made impossible.

Electoral College A group of representatives from each of the states who meet and vote for a particular candidate.

electoral votes Votes in the Electoral College; the number of electoral votes a state has is based on the number of senators and representatives it has.

homesteading Historically related to the Homestead Act of 1862, which allowed a settler who had cleared and worked land for five years to receive a title to the land from the government; helped promote settlement of the American West in the nineteenth century.

impeach To bring an accusation against someone.

party platform The stated goals and policies of a political party.

progressive Favoring change, improvement, or reform.

Reconstruction The plan for recovery and rebuilding the nation after the Civil War.

secede To leave or withdraw from a group or organization; used to describe the decision of Southern states to leave the Union shortly before the Civil War.

tariff A tax placed mainly on imported goods, designed to protect a country's businesses, industries, and manufacturers from foreign competition.

temperance movement A movement that called for the strict regulation of or banning of sales of alcoholic beverages.

veto power The power to block laws or agreements; the president has the power to veto a bill passed by Congress; this power cannot be used to block constitutional amendments, and Congress can override the president's veto with the support of two-thirds of both the Senate and the House of Representatives.

BIBLIOGRAPHY

Binkley, Wilfred E. *American Political Parties*. New York: Alfred A. Knopf, 1962.

Bjerre-Poulsen, Niels. *Right Face: Organizing the American Conservative Movement, 1945–65*. Copenhagen, Denmark: Museum Tusculanum Press, 2002.

Foner, Eric. *Free Soil, Free Labor, Free Men: The Ideology of the Republican Party Before the Civil War*. New York: Oxford University Press, 1970.

Gerring, John. *Party Ideologies in America, 1828–1996*. New York: Cambridge University Press, 1998.

Gienapp, William E. *The Origins of the Republican Party: 1852–1856*. New York: Oxford University Press, 1987.

Gingrich, Newt. *To Renew America*. New York: HarperCollins, 1995.

Hess, Stephen, and David S. Broder. *The Republican Establishment: The Present and Future of the G.O.P.* New York: Harper & Row, 1967.

Marcus, Robert D. *Grand Old Party: Political Structure in the Gilded Age 1880–1896*. New York: Oxford University Press, 1971.

Moos, Malcolm. *The Republicans: A History of Their Party*. New York: Random House, 1956.

Myers, William Starr. *The Republican Party*. New York: Century Co., 1931.

Rae, Nicol C. *The Decline and Fall of the Liberal Republicans: From 1952 to the Present.* New York: Oxford University Press, 1989.

Reichley, A. James. *The Life of the Parties: A History of American Political Parties.* New York: Free Press, 1992.

Schneider, Gregory L. (ed.) *Conservatism in America Since 1930.* New York: New York University Press, 2003.

Stelzer, Irwin (ed.). *The Neocon Reader.* New York: Grove Press, 2004.

Web Sites

The American Presidency Project
http://www.presidency.ucsb.edu

American President: An Online Reference Resource. University of Virginia: Miller Center of Public Affairs
http://www.americanpresident.org

American Treasures of the Library of Congress
http://www.loc.gov/exhibits/treasures

C-SPAN
http://www.c-span.org

Digitas
http://www.digitas.harvard.edu

The Dwight D. Eisenhower Library
http://www.eisenhower.archives.gov

Encyclopaedia Britannica
http://www.britannica.com

GOP.com: Republican National Committee
htto://www.gop.com

The Heritage Foundation
http://www.heritage.org

Leadership Conference on Civil Rights
http://www.civilrights.org

The Living Room Candidate. American Museum of the Moving Image
http://www.livingroomcandidate.movingimage.us/election/

National Park Service
http://www.nps.gov

The President Benjamin Harrison Home
http://www.presidentbenjaminharrison.org

United States Department of Justice
http://www.usdoj.gov

U.S. National Archives and Records Administration
http://www.archives.gov

Washington Post
http://www.washingtonpost.com

FURTHER READING

Barney, William L. *The Civil War and Reconstruction: A Student Companion*. New York: Oxford University Press, 2001.

Kronenwetter, Michael. *Political Parties of the United States*. Berkeley Heights, N.J.: Enslow Publishers, 1996.

Strausser, Jeffrey. *Painless American Government*. Hauppauge, NY: Barron's Educational Series, 2004.

Web Sites

American Experience: Reconstruction: The Second Civil War
http://www.pbs.org/wgbh/amex/reconstruction/

The American Presidency
http://www.ap.grolier.com

American Treasures of the Library of Congress
http://www.loc.gov/exhibits/treasures

Elections the American Way, Library of Congress
http://www.memory.loc.gov/learn/features/election/

The White House: The Presidents of the United States
http://www.whitehouse.gov/presidents/

PICTURE CREDITS

INDEX

ABOUT THE AUTHOR

HEATHER LEHR WAGNER is a writer and an editor. She is the author of more than 30 books exploring social and political issues and focusing on the lives of prominent men and women. She earned a B.A. in political science from Duke University and an M.A. in government from the College of William and Mary. She lives with her husband and family in Pennsylvania.